How To Find Out If You Have Rejection Sensitive Dysphoria

A Methodical Approach for Identifying Intense Rejection

By John-Paul Byrne

Book #2 in the *Understanding and Identifying Rejection Sensitive Dysphoria* series.

Copyright Notice

How To Find Out If You Have Rejection Sensitive Dysphoria
A Methodical Approach for Identifying Intense Rejection

Published by John-Paul International Ltd, International House, 12 Constance Street, London, United Kingdom, E16 2DQ

ISBN: 9798645145750

www.HelpWithRSD.com

Image Cover/Credits:
Images courtesy of canva.com. Cover design by John-Paul Byrne
Last edited on: 31 May 2023

This book is dedicated to Kay for
always being there for me, our
beautiful children and your friendship.

Get The Next Book

Thank you for putting your faith in me and purchasing this book.

How To Find Out If You Have Rejection Sensitive Dysphoria
is the second book in the series
Understanding and Identifying Rejection Sensitive Dysphoria

Get the next book in this series by visiting:

www.helpwithrsd.com

I would be most grateful if you could leave a review on Amazon so that others needing help with RSD can discover this book.

I wish you inner peace, self-love and happiness in your journey with Rejection Sensitive Dysphoria

- John-Paul Byrne, Peterborough, UK

Introduction

I hope that you arrive here after reading *The Beginners Guide To Rejection Sensitive Dysphoria*, the first book in the series *Understanding and Identifying Rejection Sensitive Dysphoria*.

Rejection Sensitive Dysphoria, often shortened to RSD is a subject that fascinates me and has been part of my life.

I began writing this series of books after my ADHD (Attention Deficit Hyperactivity Disorder) diagnosis and upon further work with a mental health professional, I was told I *have* RSD.

Knowing what RSD stood for and that it is thought to be a chemical dysfunction of the brain, was certainly helpful to me. It seemed as though finally I had something to point at which explained why I had felt rejected so intensely, so often. I didn't want to blame *who* I was or abdicate personal responsibility with my new diagnosis, but it certainly provided a sound reason for what could be happening in my head.

However, I wanted to know more. I wanted to understand this condition and I wasn't ready to accept that there was nothing I could do about it. I am grateful to my partner Flavia for holding this view and encouraging me to poke and prod at this diagnosis and challenge its widely accepted guidance of "you can't do anything about it."

After all, we are in charge of our minds and our bodies. Did you know that with intention alone a person can change the pH value of water by a whole unit? I think that's quite incredible. Considering that we are mostly made up of water this suggests to me that we have the potential to re-wire our brains and perhaps even consciously affect the chemicals it produces.

If you were to ask me now, as I write this book, "Do you have RSD John-Paul?" I would say No. I think I have managed to eliminate it from my life and made huge improvements even since writing the first book. It does on occasions come up to the surface but not at the intensity or frequency of the years prior to working on myself.

Throughout this series of books, I will lead you on the path that has enabled me to say *this* in the hope that you too, can one day, overcome intense rejection.

The first step for me in working with RSD, was to really understand what was going on. I am quite a strange blend of creative and logical. I like to apply logical, simple, step-by-step approaches to complex subjects, breaking them down into manageable chunks that can easily be understood.

That's what I sought to do in this book. The first step for us together, now that we have understood the basics from the beginner's guide, is to figure out if you or someone close to you might have RSD and/or suffers from intense rejection. Whilst I did provide a simple approach in the beginner's guide, this book presents a deeper dive and rigorous methodology that I have developed.

I want to draw an important point here before we dive into my methodology together: RSD, in my view, is like an official label for intense rejection. I don't think any of us would be human if we did not feel rejected at one time or another. However, RSD is pointing at those of us who experience *intense* rejection. Remember that intense rejection can really impede on a person's happiness and well-being. They might feel rejected most of the time, waiting for the next unexpected rejection event to occur at the slightest moment, only to re-live the pain on repeat.

Before we begin, I need to remind you of what I've said at numerous junctures in these books: ***I am not a qualified mental health professional***. Whilst I am a Certified Coach, non-practising Hypnotherapist and qualified in NLP (neuro-linguistic programming) as well as Time Line Therapy, you must not assume that I am providing medical advice to circumvent qualified clinicians.

I am an ordinary person sharing my experience of what I have discovered and what has worked successfully for me. You must, and I repeat, YOU MUST ALWAYS SEEK QUALIFIED MENTAL HEALTH SUPPORT.

There is no official diagnosis for RSD but using the methodical approach I have detailed inside this book you can evaluate for yourself if you have RSD. Regardless of whether we label it as RSD or simply *intense rejection*, you will find the steps which I have created for you to follow, invaluable in finding out if you have RSD in your opinion.

In order to get the most value from this book, I would recommend that you read it cover to cover and then start again from the beginning, taking one chapter at a time. As you re-read each chapter, allow yourself the time to do the work and exercises contained within. Some of them might take you a few days to complete or even a few weeks perhaps, especially when you are logging your rejection events.

Allow yourself the time to get the most from this book and if you arrive at the conclusion that you or someone close to you, likely suffers from intense rejection, then please continue with the next book in this series. It is designed to deepen your understanding and move forward towards positive steps for reducing its effect on your well-being and happiness.

You can find other books in this series that provide strategies for living with RSD by visiting:

https://www.helpwithrsd.com

I also highly recommend purchasing the *Rejection Event Journal* in paperback from Amazon. This supports all of my books on this topic. This will really help you in moving through RSD as introduced in the beginner's guide. I created it especially for you.

Let's continue our journey with RSD together.

The RSD Wheel of Rejection Assessment™

Chapter One

I n *The Beginners Guide to RSD*, I introduced a simplified twelve question assessment that you can use to identify if you suffer from intense rejection in a disproportionate way, compared to the average person. This was fine to introduce you to RSD, but in this book, we will be diving deeper together and doing more detailed work to discover how you experience rejection.

Before we work further into the different aspects of RSD, I want you to take this more detailed assessment. It statements are grouped by the characteristics of RSD. These are the same characteristics that we will then explore in detail within the coming chapters.

The assessment is titled the **RSD Wheel of Rejection Assessment™** because at the end of assessment you can generate a visual indicator that you can use to evaluate if you suffer from RSD. The *wheel* concept is representative of how all characteristics of RSD feed off one another, rolling from one characteristic to the next, adding to the intensity of a rejection event.

You can take this assessment at any time. I hope that you find it a fantastic indicator of whether you suffer from intense rejection, akin to RSD. Just a reminder that you can also get support from someone close to you who may be able to help you complete the questions and provide a perspective different to yours.

Before you begin, I want to outline the key characteristics that this assessment focuses on. These characteristics are the sum experience of the aspects of RSD that I have identified, experienced and observed in others.

1. Emotional Intensity:

Any assessment of RSD should naturally extract indicators of the experience of strong emotions. These are emotions that are difficult to control, overwhelming and all consuming.

2. Reactions:

How we react to rejection reflects how we deal with it internally. The assessment seeks to identify physical reactions. These include verbal and physiological such as experience a shaking body, for example. The stronger we react to rejection indicates its intensity.

3. Frequency:

The frequency that someone experiences intense rejection is a strong indicator of the *dysphoric* nature of it. Remember that the *D* in *RSD* stands for *dysphoria*, an experience disproportionate to what is actually happening.

4. Looping:

Intense rejection comes with internal thought loops that can run wild and out of control. The assessment seeks to identify whether these loops exist, their impact on you and their frequency. Having a looping thought for days about a perceived or real rejection event, is a strong indicator or RSD.

5. Avoidance:

If you experience intense rejection on a regular basis, the natural defence strategy is to avoid pain and more towards comfort. This means we try to avoid situations or people where rejection could be triggered again. The assessment identifies avoidance strategies and their prevalence.

6. Validation:

Seeking validation from outside ourselves on a relentless basis is a strategy that the mind develops to gain a sense of security that future rejection events are not about to occur. The assessment will help you identify how often and how important seeking validation from others is for you.

7. Self-Loathing:

When intense rejection is triggered, it exists with self-loathing. The self-loathing justifies the experience of the rejection and is a by-product of the intense emotions. It's a way of rationalising the rejection experiences despite its negative impact on self-esteem and overall happiness and well-being. The assessment will ask you questions that aims to identify how much disproportionate self-loathing you experience.

8. Comparing:

Comparing ourselves to others is quite natural from time-to-time. However, comparing ourselves relentlessly to another as a result of experiencing intense rejection, is an indicator of poor self-esteem and an internal attempt to self-validate.

Assessment Instructions:

The assessment might should take around 10-15 minutes to complete. It does not all have to be completed in one sitting. The key to getting the best results from it is not to over-analyse your initial response to the questions. I know this might be challenging, especially if you suffer from ADHD or low self-esteem. It is a lengthy and detailed assessment for a reason: to provide as accurate an assessment result as possible so you can discover if you have RSD.

Remember that there is no right or wrong answer and that the purpose of the assessment is to help you evaluate for yourself whether you suffer from RSD and/or the intense emotional rejection characteristics it describes.

It will also be useful to name and date your assessment, since you can take it multiple times over the coming weeks and months to note your improvement as you work on yourself throughout these books.

This *RSD Wheel of Rejection Assessment™* is also available within the *Help with RSD* mobile app, on the website and as a printed PDF by visiting:

www.helpwithrsd.com

I will constantly update the digital versions of the assessment that provide statements that seek to identify the same characteristics of RSD within you, but present different statements that achieve the same thing. This is useful if you plan to take the assessment more than once so you can avoid biasing your answers based on the answer you gave the last time.

Anyway, for this printed version, you should respond to all statements with a value of 1-5 and add up your score for each section. The assessment consists of a series of statements that you indicate your level of agreement with, on a scale of 1-5.

Here is an example statement and how you might respond to it:

"I often experience racing thoughts during a conversation when someone gives me feedback."

Answer 1 if you strongly disagree and answer 5 if you strongly agree. Otherwise use 2,3,4 to indicate your level of agreement.

In the next chapter, I will show you how to correlate your scores so you can determine if you suffer from RSD.

RSD Wheel of Rejection Assessment™

Characteristic: Emotional Intensity	Agreement
#	**Statement**	**(1-5)**

#	Statement	Agreement (1-5)
1	When I receive criticism or feedback, even if it's constructive, I often feel deeply hurt and personally attacked.	
2	If someone cancels plans with me or chooses to spend time with someone else, I feel an intense sense of abandonment or rejection.	
3	When I express my thoughts or ideas and they are dismissed or ignored, I find myself feeling invalidated and unseen.	
4	If I don't receive immediate responses to my messages or calls, I tend to assume that I am being intentionally ignored or rejected.	
5	Receiving a rejection letter or email, such as a job rejection or a declined proposal, triggers overwhelming feelings of self-doubt and inadequacy.	
6	In social situations, if I perceive others forming closer bonds or excluding me, I feel an overwhelming sense of rejection and exclusion.	
7	When my partner or loved one seems emotionally distant or preoccupied, I interpret it as a sign of rejection and fear losing their love and connection.	
8	If I make a mistake or fail at something, I tend to take it as a personal rejection, feeling deeply ashamed or unworthy.	
9	Receiving a disapproving or disappointed look or comment from someone I respect can send me into a spiral of self-criticism and feelings of rejection.	
10	When I see others receiving praise, recognition, or achievements, I often feel envious and perceive it as a personal rejection of my own worth or abilities.	
	Total Score:	

Characteristic: Reactions	Agreement
#	**Statement**	**(1-5)**

#	Statement	Agreement (1-5)
1	I often find that my emotional and physical reactions to rejection are more intense than what an average person would experience.	
2	Comparing my responses to rejection with others, I believe that my reactions are disproportionate in terms of intensity.	
3	Recovering emotionally after experiencing rejection is often a difficult and prolonged process for me.	
4	People have commented on or expressed surprise at the intensity of my reactions to rejection.	
5	I tend to ruminate or dwell on past rejections long after they have occurred.	
6	I frequently experience physical symptoms such as a racing heart, shortness of breath, or muscle tension when facing rejection.	
7	Engaging in social or romantic relationships is challenging for me due to a fear of rejection or anticipation of intense emotional reactions.	
8	There are specific types of rejection that consistently elicit stronger or more pronounced reactions from me.	

9	I have found that even minor instances of rejection can trigger intense emotional and physical reactions within me.	
10	My reactions to rejection often extend beyond the initial event, impacting various aspects of my life and overall well-being.	
	Total Score:	

Characteristic: Frequency		**Agreement**
#	**Statement**	**(1-5)**
1	I often find myself encountering situations where I perceive rejection, even if it may not be intentional or explicit.	
2	Rejection is a common theme or recurring pattern in my personal or professional relationships.	
3	I frequently put myself in situations where the likelihood of experiencing rejection is high.	
4	The number of rejection experiences I encounter in a given week or month is noticeably higher than what others around me seem to experience.	
5	Rejection has become a familiar and expected part of my daily life or routine.	
6	I often feel like I am constantly on edge, anticipating or bracing myself for potential rejection in various aspects of my life.	
7	The majority of my interactions or attempts at connection result in some form of rejection or disappointment.	
8	Others have commented on the frequency with which I encounter rejection or perceive rejection where it may not be present.	
9	Rejection tends to overshadow or dominate my overall emotional landscape and can have a lasting impact on my mood and well-being.	
10	I find it challenging to recall a significant period of time in which I have not experienced some form of rejection, whether minor or significant.	
	Total Score:	

Characteristic: Looping		**Agreement**
#	**Statement**	**(1-5)**
1	Following a rejection, I often find myself replaying the event repeatedly in my mind, analysing every detail and seeking validation or explanations.	
2	I tend to get stuck in a cycle of negative self-talk and self-critical thoughts when I experience rejection.	
3	Thoughts of past rejections frequently resurface when I face new instances of rejection, intensifying my emotional response.	
4	I struggle to let go of thoughts related to rejection, and they tend to occupy a significant amount of my mental energy.	
5	Rejection often triggers a cascade of catastrophic or worst-case scenario thoughts, creating a sense of doom and hopelessness.	
6	I find it challenging to redirect my thoughts away from rejection once they start looping, as they tend to dominate my mental landscape.	

#	Statement	Agreement (1-5)
7	Rejection can trigger a barrage of self-doubt and questioning, leading to a prolonged period of overthinking and second-guessing myself.	
8	I frequently find myself ruminating on what I could have done differently or how I could have prevented the rejection, even long after it has occurred.	
9	Rejection often leads to a spiral of negative thoughts that extend beyond the specific event, affecting my overall self-esteem and confidence.	
10	I struggle to break free from the repetitive thought patterns associated with rejection, and they can persist for extended periods, impacting my daily functioning and well-being.	
	Total Score:	

Characteristic: Avoidance	Agreement
#	Statement	(1-5)
---	-----------	-------
1	I often find myself avoiding social situations or events where I perceive a risk of facing rejection.	
2	I tend to withdraw or isolate myself from others as a way to protect myself from potential rejection.	
3	I frequently make excuses or find reasons to avoid situations or interactions where I fear rejection might occur.	
4	When faced with the possibility of rejection, I have a strong inclination to retreat into my comfort zone and stick to familiar routines.	
5	I find it challenging to initiate or pursue new opportunities or relationships due to a fear of rejection.	
6	I tend to downplay or dismiss my own desires or ambitions to avoid the potential disappointment and rejection that may come with them.	
7	I often find myself avoiding confrontation or difficult conversations, as they could lead to rejection or conflict.	
8	I have a tendency to seek reassurance and validation from others as a way to minimize the risk of experiencing rejection.	
9	When faced with potential rejection, I have a tendency to engage in distracting behaviours or activities to avoid confronting the situation directly.	
10	I frequently find myself hesitating or holding back from expressing my true thoughts or feelings, fearing the potential rejection or negative reaction it may elicit.	
	Total Score:	

Characteristic: Validation	Agreement
#	Statement	(1-5)
---	-----------	-------
1	I frequently seek reassurance and validation from others to feel secure and protected against potential rejection.	
2	The opinion and approval of others hold significant weight in how I perceive my own self-worth and value.	
3	I often rely on external validation as a way to validate my own thoughts, feelings, and decisions.	

4	I find myself constantly seeking feedback and validation from others, even for minor or inconsequential matters.	
5	Receiving compliments and praise from others plays a vital role in boosting my self-esteem and reducing the fear of future rejection.	
6	I have a strong desire to be liked and accepted by others, and I feel uneasy when I sense any potential signs of disapproval or rejection.	
7	Seeking validation has become a constant and automatic response to any doubts or insecurities that arise within me.	
8	I prioritize external validation over my own internal compass when making decisions or taking action.	
9	I often compare myself to others and seek validation by measuring my worth against their achievements or social acceptance.	
10	The fear of rejection and the need for validation regularly influence my behaviour and choices, sometimes leading to compromising my own values or needs.	
Total Score:		

Characteristic: Self-Loathing		Agreement
#	**Statement**	**(1-5)**
1	When I face rejection, I often engage in self-critical thoughts that reinforce a sense of self-loathing.	
2	I find it difficult to separate my self-worth from the rejection I experience, leading to feelings of self-loathing.	
3	The intensity of my emotional response to rejection often fuels negative internal dialogue, as I blame myself excessively for the outcome.	
4	I tend to internalize rejection as a personal flaw or failure.	
5	Moments of rejection amplify my negative self-talk, making it challenging to maintain a positive self-perception.	
6	I frequently find myself in a cycle of self-loathing, where rejection experiences reinforce negative beliefs about myself.	
7	My experience of rejection can trigger a cascade of negative thoughts about myself that linger long after the event has passed.	
8	I struggle to separate my value as a person from the rejection.	
9	The intensity of my self-loathing in response to rejection often exceeds what others might consider a reasonable or proportionate response.	
10	I recognize that self-loathing negatively impacts my self-esteem and overall happiness, but breaking free from this pattern is challenging.	
Total Score:		

Characteristic: Comparing		Agreement
#	**Statement**	**(1-5)**
1	After experiencing rejection, I frequently find myself comparing my worth and accomplishments to those of others.	
2	I have a tendency to constantly measure my self-worth based on the achievements and successes of others.	

3	The experience of rejection often leads me to engage in relentless comparisons with others, seeking validation and self-justification.	
4	I find it challenging to resist the urge to compare myself to others after facing rejection, even though it negatively affects my self-esteem.	
5	Comparing myself to others is a way for me to try to validate myself and prove my worthiness despite the impact of rejection.	
6	I often catch myself obsessively scrolling through social media, comparing my life to the curated highlight reels of others, especially when I'm feeling the effects of intense rejection.	
7	The comparisons I make with others after experiencing intense rejection are indicative of underlying issues with my self-esteem and self-validation.	
8	I tend to focus on the achievements or attributes of others that I perceive as superior, which intensifies my self-doubt and feelings of inadequacy.	
9	The frequency and intensity of my comparisons with others increase significantly after facing rejection, as if trying to find evidence of my unworthiness.	
10	Comparing myself to others as a response to rejection perpetuates a cycle of negative self-perception and hinders my ability to heal and move forward.	
	Total Score:	

Well done. You have completed the *RSD Wheel of Rejection Assessment*™. You can celebrate because it takes commitment to yourself to learn new things about yourself.

In the next chapter, I will show you how to plot your results on the *Wheel of Rejection*™ so you can evaluate if you suffer from RSD.

RSD Wheel of Rejection Assessment™ - Results

Chapter Two

Now that you have completed the assessment, I want to show you how to plot your results on the Wheel of Rejection™ so you can determine if you have RSD.

You should have ended up with a total score for each RSD characteristic. An example set of scores is shown below.

Characteristic	Total Score
Emotional Intensity	34
Reactions	45
Frequency	25
Looping	48
Avoidance	23
Validation	17
Self-Loathing	38
Comparing	50
Overall Score (A):	280
Total Possible Score (B):	400 (i.e. 10 * 5 * 8)
Percentage % (A/B) * 100	70%

In the example table above, the total score from each of the characteristics have been added together, resulting in 280. If you had strongly agreed with every single statement (i.e. a 5), then the maximum score you could achieve would be 400. We then calculated that you are 70% likely to have RSD. Here is a summary table that describes how I would use the resulting percentage to discover the likelihood that you have RSD i.e. you suffer from intense dysphoric rejection.

%	Likelihood of RSD
1-30	You don't suffer from intense rejection. How you handle rejection appears not to trigger the characteristics of an RSD sufferer at any great degree.
31-70	Rejection can be difficult for you to handle but you don't quite tick all the boxes that someone who suffers with RSD would.
71-90	You highly likely suffer with RSD as a high percentage of the characteristics of RSD come into play. Episodes of rejection for you, are very difficult to handle but not out of control.
91-100	You most definitely have RSD and suffer from intense dysphoric rejection. You should seek out professional therapeutic support as you see fit.

Whilst knowing the percentage likelihood that you suffer from RSD based on the ranges from the *Wheel of Rejection Assessment™* above, it is also useful to visualise the results to get a sense of how many and how deeply each characteristic of RSD comes into play for you, when rejection occurs.

The rejection wheel can easily be completed by taking the total score of each characteristic and dividing it by ten and rounding accordingly,

You can download a printable *Wheel of Rejection™* graphic from:

www.helpwithrsd.com

Simply use the diagram shown on the next page and put a dot on the appropriate line in each segment. You can then connect all the dots and colour the enclosed area in to get a sense of the *coverage* of the characteristics.

You can use this diagram to complete your own wheel:

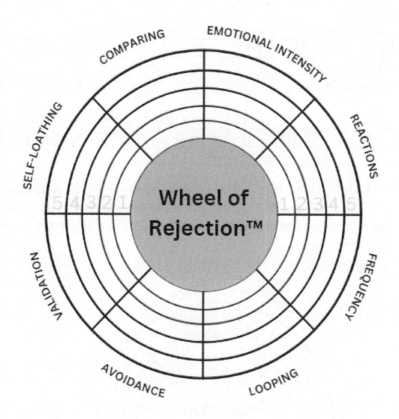

Here is an example of a wheel that shows someone who does struggle with rejection but doesn't satisfy my criteria for RSD.

Characteristic	Total Score
Emotional Intensity	45
Reactions	28
Frequency	17
Looping	17
Avoidance	47
Validation	38
Self-Loathing	8
Comparing	36
Overall Score (A):	236
Total Possible Score (B):	400 (i.e. 10 * 5 * 8)
Percentage % (A/B) * 100	59%

As you can see they fall into this description based on 59% as they are between 31-70%: *Rejection can be difficult for you to handle but you don't quite tick all the boxes that someone who suffers with RSD would.*

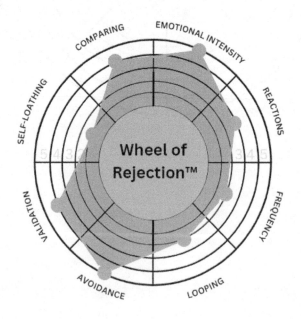

Here is an example of someone who doesn't have any indicative characteristics of RSD:

Characteristic	Total Score
Emotional Intensity	15
Reactions	12
Frequency	28
Looping	11
Avoidance	26
Validation	5
Self-Loathing	5
Comparing	7
Overall Score (A):	109
Percentage % (A/B) * 100	28%

As you can see, they fall into this description based on 28% as they are between 1-30% In this example we didn't colour in the area enclosed by connecting the dots, just to show you that it doesn't affect how you read the resulting diagram.

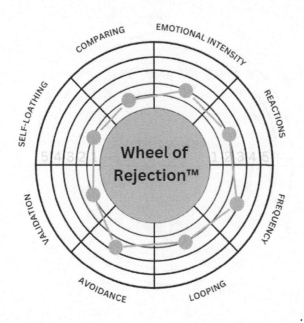

Here is an example of someone who is highly likely to suffer from Rejection Sensitive Dysphoria

Characteristic	Total Score
Emotional Intensity	48
Reactions	38
Frequency	49
Looping	19
Avoidance	50
Validation	43
Self-Loathing	44
Comparing	37
Overall Score (A):	328
Percentage % (A/B) * 100:	82%

As you can see, they fall into this description based on 82% as they are between 71-90% Notice that the enclosed area covers almost all of the characteristics that the assessment covers.

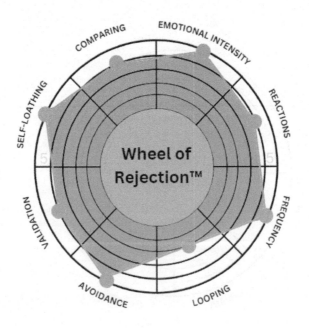

So, let us recap what we have covered in this chapter.

In Chapter Two, I introduced you to the *RSD Wheel of Rejection Assessment™* and how it covers eight key characteristics of RSD which I identified through personal experience and observation of others. The assessment consisted of statements that you answered, which indicated the strength to which that characteristic is prevalent in you.

In this chapter, I have shown you how to take the scores and compute a percentage likelihood of RSD. I have also shown you how to complete the *RSD Wheel of Rejection™* so you can visualise the coverage of RSD across each characteristic.

Please remember that there is no official diagnosis for RSD. This is the main reason why I developed the *RSD Wheel of Rejection Assessment™*. It is up to you to decide whether the results are useful to you. If they have indicated that you are highly likely suffer from RSD, then you can choose to accept or ignore your result.

If you choose to adopt the result, it means you can then move forward with the rest of this book as I explore some of these characteristics of RSD in more detail. You will then be ready for more detailed strategies for recovery by consuming later books in this series.

I hope that you have found the assessment valuable and insightful. Please leave your feedback on our Facebook page by grabbing the link from www.helpwithrsd.com.

28

Emotional Intensity Metaphors

Chapter Three

There is an art to using metaphors to communicate intense emotions. Let's be honest, it is difficult to describe how we feel on the best of days, but for those who suffer from intense rejection, the complexity and intensity of the emotions experienced can be impossible to put into words.

In this chapter we are going to explore the emotional intensity characteristic of RSD and introduce you to the ideas of use metaphors. I have written a book dedicated to this technique called How to Use Metaphors to Communicate How You Feel. This is the just one of the books in this series that you can find on the website at www.helpwithrsd.com

But for now, I want to introduce you to the concept so you understand how you can leverage metaphors to verbalise (or write down) how you feel. You can then use this understanding and knowledge to communicate your feelings to yourself and others. This will help you become more objective about rejection events that you experience and be able to recover from them faster.

This process will also work hand-in-hand with the paperback *Rejection Event Journal* that you can also find on the above website.

So, what are metaphors?

In a nutshell, metaphors are like secret codes that can convey complex emotions using simple words and images. They're great at dressing up emotions, especially the intense ones, in a way that makes it easier for you and others to understand. A metaphor doesn't just say that something IS something else; it paints a vivid picture that touches the imagination.

For instance, when you say "I feel like a deflated balloon," you're not just saying you're sad or disheartened. You're expressing a deeper sense of loss, disappointment, and exhaustion.

So why are metaphors so powerful? The answer is, they engage our brains in a way that literal language simply can't. Metaphors work like a well-placed hook in a catchy song, they draw us in, captivate our attention, and make the experience so much more enjoyable.

Metaphors engage multiple areas of our brains:

Metaphors don't just light up the language processing areas of our brains; they also activate the regions linked to sensory and motor skills. That's why when someone says, "Life is a roller coaster," you can almost feel the thrill, the ups and downs, and the adrenaline rush!

Metaphors makes abstract concepts concrete:

Emotions are complicated. Sometimes they're so abstract, it's like trying to catch smoke with your hands. But metaphors are like a solid container for that smoke. That is a metaphor isn't it! A metaphor can transform abstract emotions into tangible images, making them easier to grasp and understand.

Metaphors boost memory and understanding:

Our brains are wired to remember stories and images better than cold facts. It's like how you can easily remember the plot of your favourite movie but struggle with recalling a history lecture. Metaphors, with their vivid imagery and relatability, stick in our memory like peanut butter sticks to the roof of your mouth.

Metaphors Cultivate Empathy:

A metaphor creates a bridge of understanding between two people. When you describe your feelings using metaphors, you invite others into your emotional landscape. It's like giving them a VIP pass to your personal emotional concert. This can cultivate empathy and make others more attuned to your feelings.

Metaphors aren't just pretty phrases or linguistic decorations.

So how do we leverage metaphors to explain the emotions we experienced after *rejection event*. It's important that you take the time after journalling a rejection event, as I described in the Beginners Guide to RSD, to create metaphors around the emotions you experienced.

So, how exactly do you use metaphors to explain what's going on inside your head and heart?

Identify Your Emotion:

Be the detective with your feelings. Are you feeling sad? Angry? Frustrated? Confused? Try to label it.

Find Your Metaphor:

Think about what object, situation, or scenario can best describe how you're feeling. It could be anything from a wilting flower to a raging storm. Have fun with it!

Describe It:

Dive deeper and describe your metaphor. Are the petals of the wilting flower drooping? Is the storm tearing trees from their roots? This helps paint an even clearer picture of your emotions.

Let's look at some examples to get your creative juices flowing:

"Feeling rejected feels like a cold winter day, where the biting wind penetrates your coat and chills you to the bone."

"When criticized, it feels like being a sandcastle washed away by an unexpected wave, leaving nothing behind."

"I often feel like an old, forgotten doll in a toy shop, desperately waiting to be chosen and loved."

Remember, these are just examples. The beauty of metaphors is that they are unique to your experience.

To be able to create more effective metaphors, it is going to be useful for me to recap the core emotions that are part of the human experience.

Core Human Emotions

While there's some debate among psychologists about how many core emotions there truly are, most agree on a set of basic ones.

1. **Joy**: It's that bubbly, light-as-a-feather feeling that comes with happiness, pleasure, and satisfaction.

2. **Sadness**: It's the opposite of joy. When you feel low, disheartened, or have a sense of loss, you're experiencing sadness.

3. **Fear**: This is the heart-pounding emotion that jumps out when you sense danger or a threat. It could be physical, like a barking dog, or psychological, like the fear of failure.

4. **Disgust**: This is the "eww" feeling you get when you encounter something repulsive, unpleasant, or offensive. It's not just about

rotten food or gross bugs—it could also be moral disgust towards unfair practices.

5. **Anger**: You've probably met this fiery emotion when you've been hurt, frustrated, or experienced injustice. It's that hot, prickly feeling that can make your blood boil.

6. **Surprise**: This emotion pops up when you encounter something unexpected. It's like the gasp you give when a friend throws a surprise party for you!

7. **Trust**: This warm, comforting feeling grows when you feel safe and secure with someone or something. It's what glues relationships and communities together.

8. **Anticipation**: It's the excited buzz you feel before a big event or change. Like the night before your birthday or when you're waiting for a package to arrive.

Each of these core emotions can be experienced in different intensities, and they often mingle with each other to create more complex feelings which is what happens during episodes of intense rejection.

Also, remember that no emotion is inherently "good" or "bad"— they all are an essential part of the human experience.

I hope that this introduction to using metaphors for describing the complexity of intense emotions that you experience during rejection, proves valuable to you.

Rejection Event Frequency Evaluation

Chapter Four

I n this chapter I will be showing you how to assess the frequency of your rejection events. Throughout this book, I will refer to *You* and *Your* but if you are reading this book for someone else, then that's ok too, you can still follow along and do the exercises with them.

So why is it important to know the frequency of your rejection events in order to assess if you might suffer from intense rejection?

The average person does not experience intense rejection that often. Perhaps when declined for that promotion, turned down for a date or had their business idea poo-pooed, then these events might be the cause for some feelings of rejection. Those life events which can make us feel rejected don't happen all that often to the average person.

The fact that you are reading this book means that you are already *aware* of rejection sensitive dysphoria as a *thing, a condition* or however you wish to refer to it. This is important because, I found, that the first step to being objective about how I was feeling, what was triggering me and how often it was occurring was separating the *me* from *it.*

What do I mean by this?

Ironically, the only way to face RSD head on is to *not* make it about yourself. Whilst I dedicate a whole book on *How To Accept You Have RSD*, the first step is just deciding that *how* you feel is not *yet* within your control under certain conditions. You must begin to treat

RSD as separate to who you are as a person. You are not RSD or intense rejection. I want you to take a moment with this thought.

You are not RSD. You are not intense rejection. There is nothing wrong with the core of who you are.

There are patterns in your brain that trigger intense emotional responses, chemical responses, that you have not yet learnt to manage and for the moment, that's OK.

You are a good person.

Let's play a small game. Imagine you are an oak tree. You are a few hundred years old with plenty of branches and acorns and healthy-looking leaves.

Now ask yourself:

How many people dislike you?

What's your answer?

It's either going to be, *I don't know* or *None*.

An oak tree cannot be rejected yet it is alive, because it is simply an oak tree. It is unique as a tree, among other trees and no other oak tree is exactly like it. If the oak tree has some trouble with an infection on its leaves or some decaying bark or a broken branch, it is still an oak tree. It can consider the decay or the infection as a thing that is hindering its growth, but it is not a tree of decay or infection. It is still a mighty oak tree.

So, place *intense rejection,* the RSD label outside of yourself. You can visual it in a box outside of your body as though you are looking at it. This is called disassociation and it's going to serve you well and prevent you from beating yourself up every time a rejection event occurs.

Imagine there is water inside your *external box of RSD.* You are holding the box. The box is outside you always, obviously, because it's a box. However, now and again, without warning, you stumble and the water spills out of the box on your clothes. The water spilling out of the box is like a rejection event. You brain *spills* too many chemicals into your system before you have time to put a space between how you instantaneously perceive an event and logically what is actually happening.

I hope these analogies will help you separate intense rejection from who you are so that when you log the frequency of your rejection events, you will not be tempted to berate yourself or go into a loop of *I'm not good enough.*

I highly recommend grabbing the *Rejection Event Journal* from the website, www.helpwithrsd.com as this will help you log the frequency you experience intense emotional rejection.

Recap: What is a rejection event?

For the purposes of our discussion, a *rejection event* are moments when you feel intensely rejected. In *The Beginners Guide to RSD,* I describe some of the feelings you might experience during a rejection event and the internal dialogue that might spiral out of control without warning.

A rejection event are those moments of intense rejection, when something has happened or been said to you or perhaps even something that you are assuming, that cause you to feel intensely rejected, perhaps worthless, perhaps angry or unwanted. Later in this book I will be taking you through a process to use metaphors to describe the intensity of your emotions, but for now you can be sure, that a rejection event are those moments when you feel intensely rejected.

You know the one: instant sick to your stomach, instantly angry, instant loss of perception, feeling like you have been discarded and so on.

Why is frequency important?

In my experience, the frequency (i.e. how often) you feel rejected, is a real indicator of intense rejection. If you are feeling rejected now and again, maybe once a week or a couple of times a month, in my view, I would say that's probably normal.

When you start to take notice how of often you feel rejected, you will be shocked at how much of your life you spend dealing with rejection. Listening to your inner self-talk is like tuning into a radio station that's broadcasting your thoughts and feelings 24/7. When dealing with RSD, this station might often play the "I've been rejected" track. Your job is to figure out how often this track is on repeat.

To do this, start by dedicating a few moments each day to check in with your thoughts. What are they saying? How are they making you feel? Do they make you feel like you've been rejected or criticized? Paying attention to these details is like taking a step back and realizing how often the rejection playlist is on a loop.

Understanding this frequency is crucial because it helps you gauge the scale of the problem and paves the way for coping strategies. It's like knowing the size of the dragon you're about to slay. Everyone's inner self-talk is unique. There's no right or wrong, too much or too little. It's about understanding your patterns and rhythm. Awareness is the first, and often, the most significant step towards change.

So, are you ready to tune into your radio station?

I put together some examples of internal dialogues that might occur when you feel rejected. It's important to remember, though, everyone's inner voice is unique, and these are just possible examples:

Why do I always mess things up? No wonder they don't want me around.

I must have said something wrong again. They looked so annoyed with me.

I knew it. I'm just not good enough. They've found someone better.

They didn't include me because they probably don't like me.

I am a burden to them. That's why they avoid spending time with me.

I can't do anything right. They must think I'm a failure.

They didn't respond to my message. They must be upset with me.

Why do I even try? I just end up getting rejected.

They laughed when I tripped. They must think I'm a joke.

I didn't get invited to the party. They probably don't want me there.

When you catch yourself having these kinds of self-talk, it's important to challenge them with compassion and understanding. Rejection often says more about the situation or the other person than about you.

If you are experiencing rejection multiple times per day, then that is disproportionate and if you have already taken the RSD Wheel of Rejection Assessment™ you will know the likelihood of whether you already suffer with RSD.

Before we move on, a question to consider is:

Should I tell the other person every time I feel rejected?

Sharing your feelings of rejection, whether using metaphors or not, can be a double-edged sword. On the upside, expressing your emotions to someone you trust can provide relief and feelings of being understood. It's like releasing a pressure valve, which can prevent emotions from building up to an explosive level. You gain a different perspective on the rejection event that seems so intense to you. Sometimes, what seems like a harsh rejection to you might appear as a simple misunderstanding to an outsider.

However, on the flip side, constantly sharing your feelings of rejection can have some drawbacks. It might inadvertently create a self-fulfilling prophecy, where you're continually looking for rejection and finding it even when it's not there. This constant focus on negative feelings can be emotionally exhausting for both you and the person you're confiding in. Plus, it could inadvertently put a strain on your relationship, especially if the other person starts feeling overwhelmed or unsure of how to help.

I would consider sharing your feelings using metaphors described in the previous chapter, but also invest time in developing self-soothing techniques and re-framing negative self-talk. If you feel you have someone close to you who you can trust and understands that you often feel rejected, you can experiment sharing your feelings with them using the metaphors you have created.

Physical Response Mapping

Chapter Five

O ne of the things that always surprised me the most during moments of intense rejection was the physical responses in the body to the perception of the situation. These responses were often uncontrollable, but what was causing them. I would shake uncontrollably, have a thumping heart and my lips would stick to my teeth.

My aim for you in this chapter is to help you chart the responses triggered within you by the intense emotions experienced during rejection.

Why is it important to do this and how does it help in understanding if you do indeed suffer from RSD?

Assuming you have done the *RSD Wheel of Rejection Assessment™* you should have a good idea by now whether you suffer from intense rejection. One of the characteristics of RSD that the assessment focused on was our *reactions* to rejection perceived or real. These reactions include our physical responses.

So, identifying if you have a physical response to intense rejection is going to help you develop a deeper sense of whether you suffer from RSD.

The key here is to understand that you are developing an awareness of physical responses that you typically have. Your physical responses may well be different to mine, but knowing what yours are will help you recognise when you are experiencing rejection.

For example:

"Why am I shaking uncontrollably because he/she said...?"

Your physical responses can then also become a cue for you to say to yourself:

"hey, something intense is going on here right now, so maybe I can just step back a little as I am most likely going into intense rejection"

Understanding the Body-Emotion Connection

So, I want to explore the link between our emotions and our bodies, with You. Emotions, especially those linked with intense rejection, can manifest physically. Our bodies are giving us indicators of our emotional state.

Have there been moments of fear or anxiety when your heart pounded faster? Or times when your palms became damp? These physical reactions are signals, indicating the presence of strong emotions. In this dialogue between body and emotions, your body communicates its distress in a profound, yet silent, manner.

The relationship between body and emotions isn't one-directional. Your emotions can trigger physical changes, while your physical state can also impact your emotions. For instance, shallow, quick breathing can increase feelings of anxiety, while deeper, slower breaths can have a calming effect.

Understanding this connection is important for you when navigating the intense emotions associated with RSD. By recognizing the physical signs that accompany these emotions, you gain insight into your emotional state. This awareness won't make the discomfort of rejection disappear, but it will help you to manage your feelings more effectively.

As you become more in-tune to your body's reactions, you build a deeper understanding of yourself. This understanding lays the foundation for creating strategies to cope with the emotional turbulence caused by intense rejection. Recognizing and acknowledging your body's responses are important steps in this process.

The connection between your emotions and your body is a powerful one, with each element responding to the other. Understanding this connection and recognizing your unique physical responses to emotions shows that you are taking personal responsibility for your emotions and experiences of rejection.

Basic Physiology of Emotional Response

Considering the physiological aspect of emotional responses can provide us with a better understanding of what is happening to us during a *rejection event.*

To better understand the body's responses, it's worth knowing the role of the nervous system. It has two significant components that come into play: the sympathetic and parasympathetic systems. The sympathetic system activates the 'fight or flight' response when dealing with stressful situations. This activation can result in symptoms such as rapid breathing, increased heart rate, and heightened alertness.

On the other hand, the parasympathetic system is responsible for the 'rest and digest' state. It calms the body down after a stressful event, slowing the heart rate and returning the body to a state of equilibrium. It's like a built-in system for restoring balance after emotional upheaval.

So, when faced with intense emotions such as rejection, the sympathetic system might kick into high gear, leading to a cascade of physical symptoms. Paying attention to these symptoms can tell you about the intensity of your emotional response.

Additionally, the body uses various hormones, like cortisol and adrenaline, to manage stressful situations. These hormones can induce physical changes such as increased heart rate, elevated blood pressure, and heightened awareness. By recognizing these changes, you can build a better understanding of your emotional state.

Using the *Rejection Event Journal* (visit www.helpwithrsd.com) will help you in tracking the physical responses and emotional states of your rejection events.

Lastly, everyone's physiological response is unique, and it's important to note that different emotions can evoke different responses. For instance, fear might cause a cold sweat, while anger might result in flushed skin.

So, by understanding these physiological responses and their relationship with our emotions, you can more easily understand your body's signals. This understanding will help you develop more effective strategies to manage intense emotions that occur in RSD.

Mapping Core Emotions to Physical Responses

So, as you probably know by now, I like to present simple methods for conceptualising and dealing with complex things. I want to show you how to map your core emotions to the actual physical experience you have, during a rejection event.

But first, understanding the connection between our emotions and physical responses will be easier by looking at specific examples. Let's look at the core human emotions we mentioned earlier, such as fear, sadness, and anger, all of which can be stirred by rejection, and see how they can manifest physically.

Fear, often the first response to rejection, can trigger a range of physical responses. These might include a racing heart, shortness of breath, or a feeling of tightness in the chest. Your body is preparing for a 'fight or flight' reaction.

Sadness, another common emotion tied to rejection, could bring about changes like a decrease in energy, a feeling of heaviness, or even disruptions in sleep patterns. It's the body's way of encouraging us to slow down and process our feelings.

Then there's **anger**, which may result from repeated experiences of rejection. Physically, you might feel heat rushing to your face, your heart pounding, or your hands clenching. These are signs your body is gearing up to confront the issue.

Building a more comprehensive map of emotions involves considering a broader range of emotional responses. Along with fear, sadness, and anger, there are several other core emotions like surprise, disgust, and joy, which, although less frequently, can also be linked with experiences of rejection.

Surprise, for instance, can occur when rejection is unexpected. This emotion may trigger a sudden intake of breath, widened eyes, or even a gasp. Your body is signalling the need to take in new information quickly.

Disgust is another emotion that may arise in certain rejection scenarios. You might feel your nose wrinkling, a bitter taste in your mouth, or a churn in your stomach. These reactions can be your body's way of expressing distaste or repulsion.

Joy, on the other hand, may seem out of place in a discussion about rejection. However, instances where anticipated rejection does not occur can certainly elicit joy. Physically, this might manifest as relaxed muscles, a lightness in the chest, or an involuntary smile.

As daft as it sounds, I have been known to laugh as an involuntary reaction to rejection. How strange is that!

Additionally, emotions such as **guilt**, **shame**, or **relief** can also follow experiences of rejection. Each of these emotions, too, have specific physical responses that are worth noting and understanding.

By broadening the scope of emotions and their associated physical responses, we can improve our understanding of our body's language. This expanded map not only provides a useful view of our emotional landscape but also strengthens our capacity to handle the intense emotions experienced during a rejection event.

So, each emotion tends to have associated physical responses. Recognizing what yours are, is very valuable, offering insights into your emotional state. By mapping these responses, you can build a better understanding of your body's communication style, equipping you to manage your emotions more effectively.

So, here is a really simple way to build that map. Complete the table below with the physical responses you often experience during intense rejection and then write down the corresponding emotion. It doesn't matter if its an official core emotion, just write down the word that means the most to you. For example. you might use the words *scared as hell* instead of *fear*.

Physical Observation	Emotion (if I were to know)
e.g. Shaking	scared
e.g. Racing Heart	guilt

Your Response Strategy

After recognizing your unique physiological signals, the next step is creating a personalized response strategy. This involves devising ways to address the physical responses arising from rejection-induced emotions. By understanding your body's cues, you can better manage these emotions and their physical manifestations.

Your response strategy will depend largely on the physical symptoms you experience. If feelings of rejection lead to a racing heart or rapid breathing, for instance, deep breathing exercises or meditation can be effective tools to slow your heart rate and calm your breathing.

Similarly, if tension headaches or muscle tightness are your body's response to rejection, physical activity such as stretching or yoga might be beneficial. These activities not only alleviate the physical discomfort but can also help regulate emotional distress.

For upset stomach or loss of appetite, finding calming activities or relaxation techniques can be a helpful strategy. This might involve listening to soothing music, walking in nature, or engaging in a hobby that brings you joy.

You can also incorporate techniques such as cognitive-behavioral strategies or mindfulness into your response plan. These approaches can help you address the underlying emotions tied to your physical symptoms, promoting a healthier emotional state.

Your personalized response strategy is a dynamic plan that can be modified as needed. As you grow and your understanding of your body-emotion connection evolves, your strategies may need to adjust too. This adaptability is a strength, allowing you to continually refine your approach based on your current needs.

By proactively addressing your physical symptoms, you're not only managing the immediate discomfort but also acknowledging and validating your emotional experience. This process fosters a nurturing relationship with yourself, enabling you to handle intense emotions with increased resilience and self-compassion.

I hope that you have found this exploration of how the intense emotions you experience with RSD can be mapped to physical responses and then how you can leverage the physical cues to develop further clarity as to whether you suffer with RSD.

Perceived or Real

Chapter Six

What of anything is actually real? We observe the world through our eyes, interacting with our senses. For neuro-typical people, achieving balance between what is actually happening around them and how they perceive those events, is normally closely related. For someone experiencing the intense emotions of rejection, the perception of what they are experiencing is often different to what is happening in front of them.

So, throughout this book we have been helping you identify if you suffer from RSD by exploring the characteristics of it. Many of those characteristics are driven by our perception of rejection.

For example, if perceive that you are being rejected it could trigger self-loathing, avoidance strategies and looping. It's important therefore that we take some time to consider how your perception might be providing strong indicators that you suffer from RSD, as well as developing awareness about perception versus reality.

I am not saying that everyone who experiences intense rejection is out of touch with reality, instead we are exploring how our perception of rejection is out of sync with any actual rejection.

Imagine your partner said: "I don't like that dress on you". For someone with RSD, this could trigger an intense rejection event, but in reality, it's just a comment which when said to someone who doesn't suffer from intense rejection, they would probably respond with. "Well, I like it" or "Which dress do you prefer".

It's important that we try to distinguish between the event of rejection itself and our perception of that event. These two aren't always identical. Our mind is a complex entity and its interpretation of experiences can significantly shape our reality. This is particularly obvious when dealing with emotionally intense experiences such as rejection. Let's explore how intense feelings of rejection might distort our perception of reality and how we might separate the perceived from the actual. By doing this, you might discover new insights about your personal experiences and how your perception colours them.

What is Perception?

Perception, simply put, is our interpretation of the world around us. It's how we make sense of our experiences, guided by our senses, emotions, thoughts, past experiences, and even our cultural and social contexts. The process of perception is complex, involving numerous cognitive and neurological processes that work together to form our understanding and interpretation of events.

In the context of rejection, our perception plays a significant role. It influences not just how we understand the event of rejection, but also how we respond to it. For example, consider two individuals who didn't get a job they applied for. One might perceive this as a personal failure and feel intensely rejected. In contrast, the other might see it as a minor setback and an opportunity for growth.

Perception, in this sense, significantly influences our emotional response. This is because our brain tends to create narratives around our experiences, and these narratives, fuelled by our emotions, shape our perception. When dealing with an emotionally intense experience like rejection, these narratives can be particularly powerful, often blurring the lines between what's perceived and what's real.

How does rejection impact our perceptions?

When we experience rejection, our mind often goes into a protective mode, attempting to make sense of this painful experience. This process can amplify our negative emotions and create a distorted perception of the event and of ourselves.

This distortion may lead us to perceive rejection where it may not exist, or interpret neutral situations as rejecting. For instance, a friend not responding immediately to a text message might be perceived as rejection. Here, the actual event – a friend not responding immediately – is seen through a lens tinted with the fear and anticipation of rejection. This results in a perceived rejection that may not align with reality.

Intense feelings of rejection might also lead us to overgeneralize, taking a specific event of rejection and applying it broadly. For instance, getting rejected in a job interview might lead to thoughts like, "I'm always a failure" or "No one will ever hire me". These perceptions paint a reality that is broader and more absolute than the actual event warrants.

Examples of Perceived vs. Real Rejection

To illustrate the difference between perceived and actual rejection, let's consider some common scenarios. Imagine you're at a social gathering, and a friend seems to spend more time chatting with others than with you. The reality of the situation might be that the friend is simply catching up with people they haven't seen in a while. However, under the influence of intense rejection feelings, you might perceive this as them avoiding you or preferring the company of others.

Or, consider a situation where your idea is not selected in a team meeting at work. The reality could be that there were several good ideas, and the one that fit the project best was chosen. However, if your mind is clouded by rejection, you might perceive this as a personal slight, interpreting it as your team not valuing your contributions.

By understanding the difference between these perceived and real scenarios of rejection, you start to recognize the influence of your perceptions and the narratives they create.

Self-Reflection and Awareness

Building self-awareness is key to distinguishing between perceived and actual rejection. A mindful approach can be quite helpful here. When an event triggers feelings of rejection, instead of immediately reacting, pause and ask yourself, "Is this rejection real, or is it my perception? What evidence do I have?"

Keeping a journal such as by using the *Rejection Event Journal* can also be beneficial. When you feel rejected, write about the event, your feelings, and why you believe you were rejected. Later, when your emotions have settled, revisit the entry and objectively evaluate if the rejection was real or perceived.

Over time, these practices can help you become more aware of your thought patterns, perceptions, and emotional responses, offering valuable insights into your personal experiences of rejection.

Discerning Perception from Reality

Once you've built a strong foundation of self-awareness, you can start to actively discern perception from reality. One useful technique is reality-checking. When you experience feelings of rejection, check the facts. What actually happened? Try to separate the facts from your emotions and assumptions.

Another method is seeking external perspectives. Discussing your experiences with trusted friends or a mental health professional can provide alternative viewpoints and help you understand the situation more objectively.

Cognitive restructuring techniques, often used in cognitive-behavioural therapy, can also be effective. This involves identifying and challenging irrational or negative thoughts and beliefs, and replacing them with more rational, balanced views.

Coping with Perceived Rejection

Dealing with perceived rejection involves both managing the intense emotions triggered and altering the perception itself. Emotional regulation techniques, such as deep breathing, mindfulness, and physical activity, can help manage emotional distress.

To alter the perception, cognitive techniques can be effective. This includes reframing negative thoughts, focusing on positive aspects, and practicing self-compassion. Remember, it's okay to feel hurt by perceived rejection. It doesn't make your feelings less valid. What matters is how you cope with these feelings and work on shifting your perception to align more with reality.

Rejection, whether perceived or real, can be a difficult experience. But with awareness, understanding, and effective strategies, you can navigate through it with resilience, creating a healthier relationship with yourself and your perceptions.

Avoidance Strategies

Chapter Seven

When faced with experiences that might lead to rejection, it's quite natural for us to try to protect ourselves. One way we often do this is by using avoidance strategies.

So, what are avoidance strategies in the context of RSD?

The are behaviours or tactics we use to sidestep situations that we think might lead to emotional distress or discomfort, such as intense rejection. This is our mind's way of safeguarding our emotional wellbeing. However, these strategies could limit your opportunities, hinder your relationships, and stall your personal growth, especially if heavily rely on them.

By understanding what these strategies are and why we use them, we can learn to manage them effectively and develop healthier ways of dealing with potential rejection.

Avoidance and Fear of Rejection

Avoidance strategies and fear of rejection are closely linked. The thought of being rejected can be incredibly daunting, particularly for those of us who are highly sensitive to rejection. This fear can trigger a protective response, pushing us to avoid situations where we might experience rejection.

For example, you might decline invitations to social events because you're worried you won't fit in, or you might avoid asking for help because you're concerned about being seen as incompetent. In both scenarios, the underlying fear of rejection is driving the avoidance behaviour.

Do you recognise any of these patterns in yourself?

Remember, that avoidance is one of the characteristics that we evaluated when you took the *RSD Wheel of Rejection Assessment™*. This chapter will add further clarity as to whether you suffer from RSD based on the results of your assessment, together with giving you a deeper understanding about avoidance strategies that might resonate with how you are behaving.

This relationship between avoidance and fear of rejection isn't just about running away from unpleasant experiences. It's also about striving for a sense of safety and acceptance. When we use avoidance strategies, we're trying to create a reality where we're less likely to face rejection - a place where we feel secure and accepted.

Common Examples of Avoidance Strategies

Avoidance strategies can take many forms, and they can be quite subtle, making them challenging to identify. Here are some examples to give you an idea:

- **Procrastination:** This involves putting off tasks that might potentially lead to rejection or criticism. For instance, you might delay submitting a project at work because you're anxious about receiving negative feedback.

- **Withdrawal from social situations**: If you're worried about being rejected in social settings, you might limit your social interactions. You might decline invitations, avoid initiating conversations, or remain quiet in group discussions.

- **Overcompensating in relationships**: You might strive to be overly accommodating or agreeable in relationships to avoid conflicts that could lead to rejection. You might find yourself agreeing with others even when you don't genuinely share their opinions, or going out of your way to please them.

- **Not voicing your needs:** Fear of rejection might hold you back from expressing your needs and wants. You might worry that others might reject you if you appear demanding or needy.

- **Avoiding new opportunities:** You might hesitate to try new things, like applying for a promotion or starting a new hobby, due to fear of failure and subsequent rejection.

Recognizing these behaviours in yourself is the first step toward managing your avoidance strategies.

The Psychology Behind Avoidance

To effectively address our avoidance strategies, it's helpful to understand the psychological processes underlying them. Avoidance behaviour is largely driven by a psychological concept known as negative reinforcement. Negative reinforcement occurs when the removal of an unpleasant stimulus (like fear or anxiety) reinforces a particular behaviour (like avoidance). So, when we avoid situations that might lead to rejection, we experience a temporary relief from fear and anxiety. This relief strengthens the avoidance behaviour, making us more likely to repeat it in the future.

Another psychological factor at play is the self-fulfilling prophecy, where our beliefs and expectations unconsciously influence our actions, leading to outcomes that confirm those beliefs. For example, if we expect to be rejected, we might unconsciously behave in ways that bring about rejection, thereby confirming our initial belief.

Understanding these psychological principles allows us to see that while our avoidance strategies might offer short-term relief, they can reinforce our fears and insecurities in the long term. But remember, we're not powerless against these patterns. By recognizing and understanding them, we equip ourselves with the tools to break free from them.

Identifying Your Avoidance Strategies

Now that you have a grasp on what avoidance strategies are and why you might be using them, it's time to start identifying your personal strategies. This step is essential as it enables you to understand when and why you use avoidance, helping you break the cycle.

A first step in this process could be self-reflection. Take some quiet moments for yourself and think about times when you've felt intense fear of rejection. What did you do in response to those feelings? Did you withdraw, procrastinate, or overcompensate?

Keeping a journal can also be useful. Every day, make a note of any situations where you felt the urge to use an avoidance strategy. Write down the situation, how you felt, and what you did in response. Over time, you may start to notice patterns in your behaviour that you hadn't seen before.

Remember, this process isn't about judging yourself; it's about understanding yourself better. So, approach it with curiosity and kindness.

Impact of Avoidance Strategies

As you've probably figured out by now, while avoidance strategies might help you dodge feelings of rejection in the short term, they often aren't beneficial in the long run. Yes, they can provide a temporary sense of relief from anxiety or fear, but they don't help you address or overcome these feelings.

Over time, reliance on avoidance strategies can lead to a cycle where you feel increasing fear and anxiety, leading you to avoid more, which in turn reinforces your fears. This cycle can limit your opportunities for personal growth, harm your relationships, and negatively impact your self-esteem and self-confidence.

Moreover, constantly avoiding potential rejection can mean you miss out on experiences and opportunities that could lead to personal growth, improved skills, or deeper connections with others.

Alternatives to Avoidance

While it's clear that avoidance strategies aren't the best response to fear of rejection, there are healthier alternatives. These approaches focus on confronting the fear of rejection directly, developing resilience, and boosting self-esteem.

One such approach is mindfulness, which involves staying present in the moment and accepting your thoughts and feelings without judgment. When faced with potential rejection, instead of resorting to avoidance, you can observe and acknowledge your feelings of fear and anxiety. This awareness can lessen the power these emotions have over you and help you respond in a healthier way.

Another approach is cognitive reframing, which involves changing the way you interpret and think about a situation. For example, instead of viewing a potential rejection as a threat, you could view it as an opportunity for learning and growth.

If you commit to building your self-esteem and have compassion for yourself, you can become more resilient to potential rejection. This might involve acknowledging your strengths, practicing self-care, and reminding yourself that everyone experiences rejection and it doesn't reflect your worth or value.

Making a Personalized Plan to Overcome Avoidance

Now that you understand your avoidance strategies and have some alternatives in mind, it's time to put this knowledge into action. You can do this by creating a personalized plan to overcome your avoidance behaviour.

Start by identifying the situations where you tend to use avoidance strategies. Then, choose one or two alternatives that you think could work for you in these situations. Make a plan for how you'll implement these alternatives the next time you're faced with potential rejection.

Changing long-standing behaviour patterns takes time and patience. You might not get it right every time, and that's okay. What's important is that you're making a conscious effort to break the cycle of avoidance and fear.

I hope that this chapter has provided you with a further opportunity to recognise if you suffer from RSD by looking more deeply at one of its characteristics – avoidance.

Personal Impact Analysis

Chapter Eight

As we approach the end of this stage of your journey in identifying if you have RSD, it felt right to help you understand how intense rejection affects you at a personal level. The goal here isn't to place blame or dwell on negatives. Instead, it's about developing self-awareness, developing empathy for yourself, and gaining insight into how you can shape a healthier future.

In this chapter, I take a look at how the fear of rejection might be influencing your life - from your self-perception and relationships to your decision-making and health. As you read, bear in our mind that everyone's experience is unique, and it's okay if not everything resonates with you.

Rejection and Self-Perception

We discussed perception versus reality in a previous chapter. One of the significant ways rejection can impact you is through your self-perception. It can chip away at your self-esteem, making you doubt your worth and abilities. If you often feel rejected, you might start believing that there's something fundamentally wrong with you, leading to feelings of insecurity and inadequacy.

These kinds of beliefs can affect your perspective, causing you to interpret neutral or ambiguous events as rejection. For instance, if a friend doesn't immediately respond to your message, you might assume they're ignoring you because they're displeased with you, when they might just be busy.

This altered self-perception can inadvertently lead to more experiences of rejection. If you expect to be rejected, you might behave in ways that encourage that outcome, such as withdrawing from others or acting defensively.

Effects on Relationships

Fear of rejection can significantly affect your relationships. You may find yourself avoiding closeness or commitment because of the fear that you'll be rejected once others get to know you better. You might struggle to express your feelings and needs, worrying that doing so might lead to conflict and potential rejection.

These behaviours can create distance and misunderstanding in your relationships, preventing you from forming deep, satisfying connections. They can also cause you to miss out on potential relationships because you pre-emptively reject others to avoid being rejected yourself.

In the context of existing relationships, constant worry about rejection might cause you to misinterpret your loved ones' actions, seeing rejection where there is none. This can lead to unnecessary conflict and strain the relationship.

Impact on Decision Making

Living with a persistent fear of rejection can have a considerable influence on your decision-making process. You might find yourself consistently opting for the 'safe' choice to avoid potential rejection or criticism. For example, you might decline a promotion because you're worried about the increased visibility and potential for rejection, or you might avoid expressing your opinion in group settings out of fear of being disagreed with.

This risk-avoidant behaviour can limit your opportunities for growth and fulfilment. You might miss out on exciting possibilities because of your fear, and this can lead to feelings of regret and frustration. It can also contribute to feelings of being 'stuck', as you may hesitate to make changes or take steps forward even when you're dissatisfied with your current situation.

Physical Health Consequences

Chronic stress related to fear of rejection can manifest physically, leading to various health problems. You might find it difficult to sleep, experience frequent headaches, or develop digestive problems. Over time, these issues can impact your overall health, contributing to conditions like heart disease and a weakened immune system.

Mental Health Consequences

Experiencing intense rejection can significantly impact your mental health. Anxiety is a common consequence, where you may find yourself in a constant state of worry, always waiting for the next rejection to hit. This state of hyper-vigilance can drain you emotionally, leaving you feeling fatigued and even lead to burnout.

Depression is another possible consequence of repeated experiences of intense rejection. If you often feel rejected, you might start believing that you're unlovable or worthless, leading to feelings of hopelessness and sadness. You might also lose interest in activities you used to enjoy or find it difficult to motivate yourself to get through the day.

Furthermore, intense fear of rejection can lead to social anxiety disorder, where you feel overwhelming anxiety and excessive self-consciousness in everyday social situations. You might dread social events, worry excessively about them beforehand, or avoid them entirely to prevent potential rejection.

Again, these are possibilities, not certainties. Experiencing rejection doesn't mean you will necessarily face these mental health challenges. However, being aware of these risks can help you take steps towards prevention and early intervention.

Quality of Life and Life Satisfaction

Intense fear of rejection can affect your overall quality of life and life satisfaction. When you constantly worry about rejection, it's tough to enjoy your experiences fully. You might be physically present but mentally preoccupied with fears and insecurities.

The fear of rejection can also prevent you from pursuing your passions, dreams, or goals. You might hold yourself back from opportunities because of the potential for rejection. This self-limiting behaviour can leave you feeling unfulfilled and discontented with your life.

Your relationships, career, and hobbies - aspects that significantly contribute to life satisfaction - can all be hampered by a persistent fear of rejection. By recognizing and addressing this fear, you can improve your quality of life and enhance your overall well-being.

Sex and Intimacy

When rejection seeps into a relationship, it can affect the sexual dynamics between partners. If you have intense rejection sensitivity, these impacts can be even more significant. The fear and anticipation of rejection can stir up a soup of feelings, leading to a cascade of reactions that could affect the intimacy in your relationship.

Firstly, the anticipation of rejection can lead to anxiety, which is often a roadblock to sexual desire. It can create a high-stress environment where it becomes difficult to feel comfortable and relaxed enough for sexual activity. You might find yourself preoccupied with thoughts of potential rejection, which can detract from your ability to be present and engaged in the moment.

This fear could make it challenging to communicate openly about sexual desires and boundaries. Effective communication is a critical aspect of a fulfilling sexual relationship, and when clouded by the fear of rejection, it could lead to dissatisfaction and misunderstanding. You might suppress your own desires, fearing that expressing them might lead to rejection by your partner.

Rejection in a sexual context could also lead to reduced self-esteem and body image issues. Sexuality is closely linked with vulnerability and acceptance. Experiencing rejection, whether perceived or real, might make you question your attractiveness or desirability, which could further affect your sexual confidence and enjoyment.

Try to recognize these impacts and understand that it's perfectly okay to seek help. Conversations with your partner, self-love and acceptance practices, or even professional help from a therapist can assist in navigating through these challenges. Intimacy is not just about the act itself, but also about the comfort, trust, and understanding you share with your partner.

As we come to the end of this chapter, it's essential to remember that experiencing intense rejection is not a personal failing or weakness. It's a part of your journey, and every step you're taking towards understanding and healing is a testament to your strength and resilience.

Owning your story involves acknowledging your experiences, understanding their impacts, and taking steps to navigate through your fears. It's not about wiping out the fear of rejection entirely – that's an unrealistic expectation, considering that everyone, to some degree, fears rejection. Instead, it's about developing the ability to cope when the fear arises.

The process might seem challenging, and that's okay. You're not alone in this journey. There are resources and supports available to help you through it, including therapists, support groups, and self-help books. Remember, it's not only about the destination but also about the journey. Each step you take is a step towards a more empowered, resilient, and self-compassionate you.

What are my next steps with RSD?

The purpose of my writing books on RSD is to provide practical steps for sufferers so they can learn about their condition, manage it and enjoy a happier internal experience.

This book *How To Find Out If You Have Rejection Sensitive Dysphoria* **is** the second book in the series *Understanding and Identifying Rejection Sensitive Dysphoria*.

I highly recommend that you now go read the next book in the series titled *How to Identify Your Rejection Triggers.* This is a really powerful book that will help you immensely. Please can you first leave me a review on Amazon as it will really help other people who might be feeling the same as you.

If you visit www.helpwithrsd.com you can get access to:

- Other books in this series
- Rejection Event Journal
- Help with RSD mobile app
- RSD Wheel of Rejection Assessment™ printable template
- RSD Wheel of Rejection Assessment™ online assessment
- Audios and Rejection Recovery Power packs
- Help with Rejection blog ... and more useful resources!

Other series on this topic will help you grow through this condition and enjoy a happier, healthier quality of life.

Author Summary

I have really enjoyed writing this second book in the series *Understanding and Identifying Rejection Sensitive Dysphoria*. I love providing people with practical, easy-to-follow insights and it has therefore given me great excitement to present the **RSD Wheel of Assessment™** among other strategies in this book.

The purpose of this book has been to help you identify if you or someone close to you has RSD. I hope that it has achieved this aim.

Rejection is a tricky human experience with many aspects to it. Experiencing rejection at the intensity levels that we explored in this book, is no way to live your life. Your life can be so much better, living without intense rejection and enabling you to live a happier, healthier life.

Now that you have discovered whether you have RSD, I urge you to revisit this book at any time to remind yourself of the characteristics of RSD that I personally observed and worked with in order to overcome it. You can achieve this too.

RSD is not something you have to take to your grave. Make a positive choice now with your self-diagnosed results from the assessment and take the next steps to give yourself a chance to live peacefully without the constant experience of rejection.

Acknowledgements

Thank you to everyone in my life who has treated me with kindness and compassion. There are many people I would like to thank who have put themselves and their own needs aside in order to support me. They have given constant love and kindness and I am truly grateful to them.

Thank you to Lucy for all your support, love and for listening to my constant chatter.

Thank you to Flavia for your love, kindness and encouragement to discover myself and never give up. Your belief in me and constant reminder of my core being has enabled me to begin to fly and love myself.

Thank you to my wonderful friends, Chris, Mel, Nick and Isy who have always been there to pick me up every time I feel into a dark place.

To my beautiful children Bobby and Bethany, you are both a gift from the universe. You have come through your Mum and I and bring us joy and laughter every day. I can see in you both, kindness, love and compassion. I am so proud of you, not because of your achievements, but because of who you truly are. I will always be here to guide you, love you and help you on your journey. Nothing you do is ever wrong, it's all learning and growth.

To my ex-wife Kay for your kindness. You never judged me and have provided endless guidance. You protected me from others judgment and understood my mental health challenges with love and compassion. Thank you for our beautiful children and being a wonderful Mum.

To my Dad and Marianne for your love, guidance, acceptance and understanding. Thank you for being so wonderful.

Thank you to my mental health professionals and therapists. To Tamsin, Graham and Eleanor for your amazing therapy, skill and knowledge that helped me understand my *ADHD*, *Bipolar Disorder*, *Rejection Sensitive Dysphoria* and everything in between. Without you I would still be a victim of my childhood trauma. You made me feel safe and gave me the pathway to recovery and growth.

Thank you to You, the reader, for trusting me with my experience and knowledge and taking the time to listen or read my words. You give me a real sense of purpose and value by purchasing my books. I hope they help you immensely.

About the Author

John-Paul Byrne writes books on mental health, self-development, business & entrepreneurship, linguistics & communication, science fiction and spirituality.

Originally from the Republic of Ireland, he now lives in the UK with his two young children. Despite a long career in software development, he has turned to writing as a passion project, hoping to have a positive impact on others.

He is an award-winning International Speaker, Entrepreneur and a Best-Selling Co-Author.

Within his words he talks to You, the reader, as he would a friend enjoying a conversation.

These publications share his own personal experience, thoughts, strategies and ideas about mental health conditions and their effects on everyday life. He hopes they will be of benefit to those seeking clarity, understanding and simple strategies to cope, survive and thrive.

He was diagnosed with *Bipolar Disorder*, *Attention Deficit Hyperactivity Disorder (ADHD)*, and *Rejection Sensitive Dysphoria (RSD)*. He feels he has conquered all three, enabling him to help others who might be earlier on in their journey.

With a keen interest in personal development, mindset and the effects of brain dysfunction, he brings you these publications with gratitude.

You can find out more about him at www.johnpaulbyrne.com

Bibliography

This book has been influenced by other experts in the field of mental health disorders. Below are some references and sources, but not exhaustive, that have contributed to the understandings conveyed in this book.

Dr Joe Dispenza www.drjoedispenza.com

Very Well Mind: Article: What is Rejection Sensitivity? https://www.verywellmind.com/what-is-rejection-sensitivity-4682652

Psychology Today: Article: What is Rejection Sensitive Dysphoria: https://www.psychologytoday.com/gb/blog/friendship-20/201907/what-is-rejection-sensitive-dysphoria

Mark R Leary, Phd: Article: Emotional Responses to Interpersonal Rejection https://www.ncbi.nlm.nih.gov/pmc/articles/PMC4734881/

Glossary

Rejection Sensitive Dysphoria (RSD): an extreme emotional sensitivity and pain triggered by the perception that a person has been rejected or criticized.

Dysphoria: a state of unease or generalized dissatisfaction with life.

DSM-5: a manual for the assessment and diagnosis of mental health disorders used by psychiatrists and mental health clinicians.

Attention Deficit Hyperactivity Disorder (ADHD): A mental disorder of the neurodevelopmental type. It is characterized by difficulty paying attention, excessive activity and acting without regards to consequences, which are otherwise not appropriate for a person's age.

Rejection Event: a moment of perceived or real rejection.

Mental Health Disorder: a mental disorder, also called a mental illness or psychiatric disorder, is a behavioral or mental pattern that causes significant distress or impairment of personal functioning.

Appendix

Other books available in the series
Understanding and Identifying Rejection Sensitive Dysphoria
are available at https://www.helpwithrsd.com

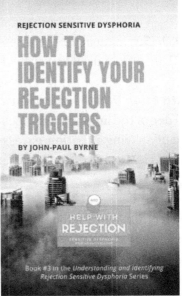

REJECTION SENSITIVE DYSPHORIA

HOW TO ACCEPT YOU HAVE REJECTION SENSITIVE DYSPHORIA

BY JOHN-PAUL BYRNE

HELP WITH
REJECTION

Book #4 in the *Understanding and Identifying Rejection Sensitive Dysphoria* Series

REJECTION SENSITIVE DYSPHORIA

HOW TO USE METAPHORS TO EXPLAIN YOUR RSD TO OTHERS

BY JOHN-PAUL BYRNE

HELP WITH
REJECTION

Book #5 in the *Understanding and Identifying Rejection Sensitive Dysphoria* Series

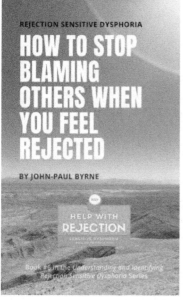

REJECTION SENSITIVE DYSPHORIA

HOW TO STOP BLAMING OTHERS WHEN YOU FEEL REJECTED

BY JOHN-PAUL BYRNE

HELP WITH
REJECTION

Book #6 in the *Understanding and Identifying Rejection Sensitive Dysphoria* Series

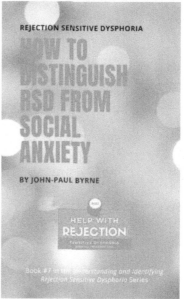

REJECTION SENSITIVE DYSPHORIA

HOW TO DISTINGUISH RSD FROM SOCIAL ANXIETY

BY JOHN-PAUL BYRNE

HELP WITH
REJECTION

Book #7 in the *Understanding and Identifying Rejection Sensitive Dysphoria* Series

Made in the USA
Las Vegas, NV
19 July 2024

92594058R00049